ELLIPSIS

Adeola Juwon Gbalajobi

First published in Great Britain as a
softback original in 2021

Copyright © Adeola Juwon Gbalajobi
The moral right of the author has been asserted.
All rights reserved.

No part of this publication may be reproduced, stored in a retrieval system, or transmitted, in any form or by any means, without the prior permission in writing of the author, nor be otherwise circulated in any form of binding or cover other than that in which it is published and without a similar condition including this condition being imposed on the subsequent purchaser.

Editing and Proofreading
Hungry Bookstore

Cover Design: Buzzdesignz

Published by 'The Roaring Lion Newcastle'
ISBN: 978-1-913636-94-4

Email:
books@theroaringlionnewcastle.com

Website:
www.theroaringlionnewcastle.com

DEDICATION

To the love to come,
the one I've been waiting for.

TABLE OF CONTENTS

ACKNOWLEDGEMENTS..1
PART 1 2
   To the Girl Who Taught Me that Ruins Can Be Beautiful ..3
   To the Girl Conjuring Butterflies in My Belly.....................4
   Almajiri 5
   King..6
   Shotgun 7
   For Amudalat Mopelade (A Poem to Trap Memories)........8
   Takotsubo..9
   For We Who Dread Love (After Michael Ace) 10
   Blessing of the Soul 11
   I Write this Poem as Sam Smith Sings *Fix You*.................12
   What is this thing your absence left 13
   Hilmi 14
   Note to a Lover 15
   Gravity..17
   Love Poems..18
   When i'm around you 19
   For Opemipo 20
   Our Love Was a Plot Twist...21
PART 2..22
   Song 001 23
   & the boy grew..24

to know to never again describe his body as a city sieged by grief 24

Portrait of My Body as Unleavened Bread 25

A Song of Repentance 26

We Are What Men Should Be When We Were Kids 27

Songbirds and Flowers 28

PART 3 29

Ìribọmi (or Baptism) 30

The Kill 31

Elegy for a Star Shawled in Dust 32

A Sutra about Fate 33

Memory as an Allotrope of Pain 34

For Ellipses 35

For Eyes that Tell Tales 36

Your sin is your skin, boy 37

Portrait of Me as a Boy with a Limped Gait 39

After the Kano Riot of 1991 40

How a Poet Grieves 41

What I Told My Friend Over the Phone When He Asked How I'm Doing 42

Song 004 43

Inertia 44

Poem for Lost Boys 46

Lullaby of Fire 47

In Search of Peace 49

On the Cliff of Mother's Tongue 50

ACKNOWLEDGEMENTS

This poet and his book wouldn't have been possible without the men and women he has encountered, who, at some point in time, poured themselves into him:

Tolu' A. Akinyemi – a stream of kindness, I am full of gratitude. Jide Badmus, thanks for all you do. Anthony Onugba, thanks for those early days; thank you to Writers Space Africa. Chinonso Ogbogu, boss and mentor, thanks for what you teach. Mrs Napa Onwusah, thanks for Shuzia! Sir Esene Charles, thanks for those conversations filled with tenderness.

Mum, Dad, Ike – my world, my universe, I love you.

Friends, thanks for your company.

To the literary platforms where some of these poems have appeared: Kalahari Review, Kreative Diadem, African Writer, Writers Space Africa, Praxis Magazine, Artmosterrific, and Ngige Review, *Asante!*

PART 1

Deny me bread, air, light, spring,

but never your laughter for I would die.

Pablo Neruda

To the Girl Who Taught Me that Ruins Can Be Beautiful

I bared my body to you –
a cosmos of ruined cities.
You packed the rubble &
built dream castles from it.
You showed me that home is made of flesh & bones –
of welcoming arms & smiles that calm storms.

To the Girl Conjuring Butterflies in My Belly

In God's earth of a million flesh &
bones, it is you my heart throbs for.

Your eyes – like stars sparkling
in the night sky –
sing the music my soul craves.

Your smile is soft & beckoning;
let me make your arms my home.

Days spent without you are like the dawn deprived of sun.
You're not here &
I'm a song with no melody.

Teach me the dialect of your heart,
the things that pull your heartstrings –
I want to be the music that tickles your ears.

Almajiri

Goodbye is stuck in my mouth like
the echo of a familiar song.
Your absence beckons the darkness.
The blinds of my heart are still
open for rays of your sunshine.
I don't know how to stop missing you,
to stop loving you;
dabs of your memories are
sewn to the helm of my mind &
I can't cut them off.
I seek the crumbs of your love –
an *almajiri* of the heart,
I'm holding on to the shadow of what once was.
I dream of roses blooming from the
shallow grave of our love;
I wake to reality – I'm terrible at giving up.

King

face set like a flint,
i come to your temple with the urgency of a burning saint –
i'm a deer panting after the water of your brook

i papered my knees at the end of the bed;
your towers spread before me like a table before my enemy,
i tongue your canaan of milk & honey

come up hither, you beckon
& my tongue responds –
traverses the expanse of your skin,
reaping broken tongues from your mouth

& now i stand at the watergate –
a muscled king, strong & mighty.
open up! & let this king come in

Shotgun

Your hair like seaweed
covers my chest
as you're cast over me –
Aphrodite over an altar of Phallus.

Our hips match the rhythm of Lil Nas X's *Old Town Road* –
You are a cowgirl riding a shotgun.

For Amudalat Mopelade (A Poem to Trap Memories)

In my dreams, you come as fireflies –
colonies of lights floating away like a lost kite in the sky.

And the more I reach,
the more the distance stretches.
Collages of archipelagos rise between us and I can't cross to you.

Ah! These paradoxes, I'm losing my mind!

I am a car speeding off on a highway and
you are a receding picture in the rearview.
But you're so with me, Amudalat,
your presence is a statement of fact.

Takotsubo

En route to *Ikeja* today, Lana Del Rey's *Cinnamon Girl* slips from the Uber's speakers, reminding me of you & the songs we used to sing till our throats burned & we quenched fire with kisses.

Cinnamon Girl was playing the day you said goodbye – words that knifed through my heart, slithering me into smithereens, the future I thought we shared slipping out of my hand like sand. Now I carry myself about like a broken effigy, a ghost of something once beautiful. *Ikeja,* a stranger smiled at me. I opened my mouth sieged by cobwebs & gave her a dry smile & walked far, far away from all the promises the smile may hold, for I know too well how it all starts – a *hello* resurrecting butterflies, blue eyes crumbling erect walls & I'm afraid I'm not whole for love again. When you left, you took a part of me along, the part meant for love & now I'm too empty to give love.

For We Who Dread Love (After Michael Ace)

In love is sometimes the distance between sanity &
madness,
being whole or broken –
why we treat love like roses grown amidst thorns,
& thread its path gently like the flap of butterfly wings.
But broken things can be beautiful too –
say, the broken mirrors that glitter
whenever the sun showers kisses on them.
We who dread love are not to blame;
wasn't death wrapped in a kiss & gifted to Christ?

Blessing of the Soul

The things that bless the soul come with no price.
Say love, say friendship,
say the gift of a hand to hold,
to walk through bitter and sweet times.

I Write this Poem as Sam Smith Sings *Fix You*

Sometimes I don't know what to do; my heart swells with so much love for you it overwhelms me; it's why in the belly of the night I wake with an ache, a longing, whispering desperate pleas into the ears of the universe that she grants me a soft landing in your heart – for grief is what shows up when you have nowhere to place your love.

This morning, the opened pages of a novel in front of me, Sam Smith's cover of Coldplay's *Fix You* slipping through the holes of my home theatre speakers *(when you love someone and it goes to waste)*, but it was our WhatsApp chats I was going through, reading through those rejections, those many rejections.

I'm learning to love you without expecting you to love me back, without asking you to. I pour my agonies into poems and sad songs instead. But sometimes I wonder what a wonder we'd made – me loving you & you loving me in return, unfurling into each other's worlds, simply being us, unaware of the miracle that we are.

What is this thing your absence left

that i've been drunk with?
See my eyes depressed by its hangover.

My heart is filled with cobwebs
(that's what happens to unoccupied spaces),
I'm keeping it for you, keeping *me* for you –
I miss you being my devotion.

I sing Lana Del Rey melancholies to sleep;
what more can sadness do to a man like me?
My roommate said I keep calling a name in my sleep.
Latifat, is that you?

Hilmi

What I do know of love is, it's
the whole of God,
the spotless liquid of his veins streaming through us –
children of flesh & blood.
It's how a stranger's name becomes our favourite song,
how a shadow's stride in the dark of night becomes
familiar,
how ageing brains still hold fresh
memories of the first kiss.

Last night, she slept off before I read her a poem.

...after my last pause, an audience roared in applause,
but my eyes were fixed on a frame
in that river of bodies that filled the hall,
hers on mine, lips tilted into a smile,
eyes sparkling with pride.

It's how we know they are the one –
they find their way into our dreams.

Note to a Lover

(To be read along with an acoustic guitar)

I'm not good at making choices.
That, I figure, is an area of strength.
It's why I'm not scared of falling & breaking,
of pouring the streams of my soul into baskets that can't hold.

I don't plan on leaving here whole.
I want tiny bits of me scattered around,
buried in people,
maybe filling up the cracked spaces in their hearts.
It means I cry too often,
but I'll be damned if there's no love to hurt.

You won't always meet me with my lips arched into a smile.
The last person that did said
it was beautiful, beautiful like fireflies in a moonless sky.
I don't laugh often either,
but when I do, it's like firecrackers spreading from the hollow pit of my belly to lighten up dark skies

(I once woke my neighbour with this thunder).

And this is me, lover:
1. a calm stream,
2. a raging sea,
3. a gloomy sky,
4. a day with a bright disposition,
5. a tender hailstorm ramming into life with all he's got.

Gravity

my body knew before you told me,
"Two months. it's Dave's…"
gravity is on the side of snowflakes;
see how they fall without breaking,
how they become bodies of water
without hurting a bone.

i swallowed words that could bruise you,
unfurled my fists into petals & led you back to the couch.

when i left you & walked into the arms of the night
with eyes humid with pain,
she welcomed me with a surety.
gravity is on my side;
see it breaking my fall so i won't hurt a bone.

Love Poems

you planted a song in my belly the first time we kissed.
at home, i wrote in my diary till my hands got sore –
my brother called it a love poem.

When i'm around you

i grin like a boy stricken stupid by Cupid's dart.
your laughter, like the soft medley of heaven's orchestra,
inspires a thousand love poems.

God is love, the holy writ says.
this miracle is all i need as proof:
how a heart stirs towards a stranger at first sight.

in the belly of the night,
i dream of your face –
the flawless cut of an artist.
your name is the song i sing when i wake.

every day holds promise because of the blessing of your smile,
abi, what is a cloudy sky compared to the
lights that gleam when you split your lips?

i'm here again in the shoes of forerunners –
Solomon, Neruda, Jide Badmus…
your love is the muse that stirs my hands.

For Opemipo

I'm dazed by the audacity of your feminine grace
& your stunning beauty.
Your confident strides
& the magic of your smile,
soft & beckoning, disarms me.

My guards are weak whenever you're close –
how you make my heart quake without knowing!

I know now how butterflies flutter in the belly –
defying the laws of gravity.
I know the chemistry of cheeks blushing red.

My eyes speak just one word whenever you're near.
I hope someday my mouth will say it.

Our Love Was a Plot Twist

These gems of memories we are so lucky to share, to collect like seashells – these silly things I remember of us: running almost naked on the seashore like naughty kids, oblivious of time and staring eyes. How we'd sit when tired, feet buried in the sand, cracking up loudly to jokes as dry as harmattan leaves, talking sentiments (like, Donald Trump is a jerk), talking about everything but us.

We loved & lusted without holding back as though our souls were aware of the mire clinging to the wheel of time, coming at us, coming at us; our love was a plot twist.

I cherish these things you left with me: the lingering scent of your perfume on the sheet, your hair scattered like grain on the pillow,

how beautiful you look with
your face wrinkled from a long night's sleep while I watch from where I am bent on the table,
writing one of those poems you hated.

I missed the powers loving you gave me, how I could turn you to a clunker of laughter & giggles while I kissed the scars where your breasts once lay.

PART 2

As the deer pants for streams of water,

so my soul pants for you, my God.

Song 001

your word is a mirror & before it, i stand juxtaposing myself,
the impurities of my heart unveiled before me.
lusts of all shades battle to darken my heart.
i turn my heart to the east &
open its blinds – flood me with light.

in the wake of dawn,
i unclad myself before you like a bride before her groom.
wash me with the water of your word & robe me with your righteousness.

how shall a young man cleanse his way?
say your word is a treasure i found in a field –
i hid it in my heart,
a rose amidst thorns.
spread, rose, spread over this garden,
fill it with beautiful fragrance
that my lover might make it his home.

& the boy grew to know to never again describe his body as a city sieged by grief

he is a piper blasting bliss from once forlorn lungs.
he throats songs of joy –
the gift the dew of morning brings.
he moulds ruins of loss into lambent dreams;
he picks joy daily from the menu of life.
failure is transient – the fleeting feet of time, he knows,
so he rams into opportunities like a bull heading for a red flag.
& the boy begins to name his body after all that's beautiful & tender.

Portrait of My Body as Unleavened Bread

For my body is bread –
I rid myself of all leaven.
Tonight, I'm a boy dousing the flame I carry in my loins.

I set myself on fire & walk with feet shod with grace –
my fragrance smells like life, like death…
heaven's harvest.

I find the strength to carry my cross from every battle
I've won (& lost)
& the remembrance of the man who bought me;
I'm a bond-slave & I'm in love with a man –

I'm sealed with his name.
Let every other lover fade away;
let other passions die on the rood of denial,
Amen!

A Song of Repentance

I come (back) to you as a suckling;
feed me the milk of your word.
Before you I'm wretched –
tanned & tattered from the sun outside your courts,
but you promise me green pastures &
still waters, bread for my weary soul.

Teacher, welts from your rod are proof of your love.
Shepherd, your staff guides me back to the fold.

Wash me with water for I'm a man of dust;
clothe me with white linen.

My soul is a whore, lover,
woo me with the sweetness of your word,
chase away other lovers & their enticements,
fill my eyes with your pleasures alone.

Your eyes are burning lamps –
they see & undo me;
flush out the greys of the night from my
inner chambers, flood me with your light!

We Are What Men Should Be When We Were Kids

"Give us out daily bread," we pray,
amidst our planning & scheming,
our wisdom that steals from us the joy of trusting

thoughts of tomorrow –
the noise that defiles the solemnity of the heart,
worries that crease our head when communing;
worry, the force that draws our knees to the ground.

We are what men should be when we were kids!

Consider the flowers of the field
or the sheep that trudge by every noon with bellies
dancing in gratitude.
Those simple things, ever trustful,
ever assured that they're in his thoughts &
he shall meet their needs.

Songbirds and Flowers

my God,
how beautiful is your world!
see the sun filtering through my blinds,
kissing me with grace, asking me to face the
day with your joy aglow in my heart.

it's morning and the garden sings of your wonder:
daffodils, snowdrops, irises – these metaphors of your beauty.
songbirds and butterflies,
trees breathing out oxygen,
they bear the trademark of your hand.

a cheerful teacher is waiting beside a school bus.
a father kisses his daughter goodbye;
her face flushes pink.
she runs to the waiting hugs of her friends.
their chatter drowns me with awe.

PART 3

There is a storm in my head...

Jide Badmus

Ìrìbọmi (or Baptism)

i

you took your eyes off the figurine on the doctor's table
&
watched a ball of water dribble down the hill of your mother's face.
she nodded as the doctor read the report in strange tongues.

after the news, you saw your body for what it was:
an animal in autothysis,
a hollow house where sadness hangs on cobwebs –
or what do you call the emptiness left by a betraying body part?
what is the word for a liver drowning in its own waters?

ii
back home, you took a walk to the sea –
you've missed her smell,
the blush on her face painted by the scarlet rays of the evening sun,
the green leaves at her side, clinging to the
helm of your skirt like the child beggars at *ipaja*.

today, the sea is calling you,
each flap of her waves an invitation to baptism.
you heed,
walk into her open arms &
join your body to the waltz of her waves.

The Kill

I had my first kill when I was six –
a butterfly with yellow and pink stripes,
fluttering over Mama's hibiscus in a May drizzle.
Clutched in my palms,
it was dead when I opened it.
Mother said that's what happens to love when we hold
too tight.

Elegy for a Star Shawled in Dust

your body
is an amalgamation of pains & scars,
a map carrying darkness, the weight of a dead child.

i see your drooling eyeballs,
i see the sorrows that depress them,
the sadness that cleaves to the roof of your tongue –

shadows loom large on you &
you are tired of breathing,
of living under the rubble of dreams.
so you court silence in the garden of broken mirrors –
mirrors dancing on your skin so your body becomes a
fountain of crimson.

your sun set at dawn –
your star shawled with dust.

A Sutra about Fate

We arrived with destiny lined in our palms –
stars wrapped in flesh & blood,

wings of dreams ready for flight,
ready to unfurl colours locked within us,

but our feathers are prey to razors &
expectations are a burden to fly with.

We're meant to be great,
but our dreams are ferried on paper boats.

Stranded on the island of despair,
where do we go from here –
do we sail backwards to straighten crooked fates?

Memory as an Allotrope of Pain

they still come to me in my dreams,
visions of limbs that become kites
flying away from their joints;
of kalashnikov seeds sowed into young bodies.
it lingers on the corridor of my nose,
the odour of bodies that became barbecue
ascending as a sacrifice to a deranged god.

a head rolled unclaimed,
the mouth that plastered kisses on a
son's lips in the morning, open in despair.

this doll belonged to my sister,
the remnant of her tiny hand still held it tight.
of her mass of flesh,
that was what was left for us to hide in the earth.

For Ellipses

Broken boys are pallid rooms full of horror.
Their skins are scriptures of scars –
the testament of waivers they got from Death.

How do you court life when Death is wooing you,
when he promises stillness to the storms in your mind?
Do you become an ellipsis –
do you choose to…

Broken boys are ellipses,
flowers that wilt in the dawn of their bloom.

For Eyes that Tell Tales

Why do your eyes tell tales
of sorrow the depth of the ocean &
joy, the expanse of the desert?

Tell me of grievances on the corridor of your eyes,
tell me the memories that make those beautiful things
glimmer.

(I know that, in the fleeting moments of our lives,
there is enough love for everyone to give,
enough joy for everyone to share &
enough sorrow for everyone to carry.)

But you, why do your eyes tell two tales at a time –
of sorrow the depth of the ocean &
joy, the expanse of the desert?

Your sin is your skin, boy

boy wearing the
face of night,
fear pumping in
his heart, hairs
coiling at the
face of light.
boy jogging to
his death – his
skin, a testament
of death, racial
profiling, fear. boy
under a knee –
george floyded.
boy in
the park, bullets
raining into his
melanin frame, boy's
body wriggling
on asphalt, the
earth sings a
dirge and his

soul gives to
it. boy whose
skin is sin,
boy whose body
breaks under the
rod of oppression,
whose body attracts
hate like shit
attracts flies. boy
vomited from home
like dysentery,
boy unsafe in
foreign lands, hunted
boy running the
streets like a
gauntlet. boy, firefly
in a sandstorm.
boy wearing the
face of night,
your skin is
your sin, boy.

Portrait of Me as a Boy with a Limped Gait

My gait is limped – flawed like a child's handwriting &
when I stand, my right shoulder slumps as though it
alone carries my depression.
My daddy, wanting to straighten me up, shouts at me to
walk like a man,
"Stop dragging those feet as though they're pregnant!"
How do I tell daddy that depression has its tentacles
around my feet,
that sorrow is a stone tied around my ankles like
bangles?
There are other secrets I carry – they're clipped to the
roof of my mouth like bats.

I have learned to tuck my scars inside my sleeves,
hide swollen eyeballs behind sunshades.
When they ask how I'm doing,
I coil my mouth into the shape of a smile &
say a practised "I'm very fine, thanks."

After the Kano Riot of 1991

father spreads his palms,
back hunched,
i plant my head in them &
he harvests my tears.
in the horizon,
the sea is swallowing the sun
like the earth, my brother's bones.
in this garden,
father and i are one in grief.
mother is somewhere among the stars,
her shadow, a dark cloud over us.
father rains tears on my head;
i look up into his eyes –
an ocean of dead things
trapping stories too heavy for his mouth to tell.

coiled on the raffia mat inside what remains of our home,
he talks about our tears in God's bottle –
son, God remembers the mourning…
i look into the night for a sign,
the face of God.
the night is empty but
at the door is
my brother, smiling at me.

How a Poet Grieves

In death may be the safest of places;
we all know loneliness is, too, where your grief &
you are cocooned from feigned cares.
This morning I wanted to pour my grief into a poem,
get some likes & comments on Instagram
while I wait for another rejection letter after it's been mailed out –
but a poem has a soul of its own, shit beamed with hope!
Who says there is light at the end of the tunnel
when my dark days are swallowed by gloomier ones?
Here I am on this couch, writing another poem,
daydreaming about colourful days I may never have.

What I Told My Friend Over the Phone When He Asked How I'm Doing

this happiness has stretched for so long, like the pacific
&
i'm afraid it'll snap back like a rubber band &
hurt me.
these days, i bounce around, leaving echoes of melodies
behind like i've got piano keys for feet,
but i'm scared my *jinns* are lurking in a corner,
waiting to pounce when the night comes.
i don't miss the darkness,
but even the brightest of days
gives way for dusk…
so, i take each joy i have in tidbits –
i'm scared to get used to things that fade.

Song 004

i

i'm a boat sailing on a sea of depression,
storms of sadness crash on me.
to balance, i've learnt to sail light –
why i let go of the burdens of love.

ii

my body is a museum of scars,
scars from slashes that sorrow might seep away,
but sorrow is the skin covering my bones.

iii

my eyes are pathways to a house of mourning – my soul.
laughter is a strange sound in this mouth.
joy is the scar on my occiput –
my eyes can't see,
my eyes can't see.

Inertia

i tilt my body on a scale,
measure myself by dreams & gifts.
every time the truth pricks me, i'm not what i should be.
it's true, the law of inertia, &
i'm the force keeping myself redundant.
isn't this one hell of an honest poem to write?

this morning, in my bed, reading, as usual,
i see all i could be if only i'm applied to it.
if only…
how we grow to become the things we detest!

i won't bother with any resolution.
the world may be ours for the taking, but
it swallows us all; there's no escaping –
it's why i don't envy the burden of world-changers,
heads buried in flurry clouds of ideas.
but we owe a debt, we owe a debt…
i don't know how best to say this.

some way, somehow, i'll be all i set out to be.
i've seen this happening like an image out of my dreams.
so, today, i torment myself with the knowledge of my emptiness,
but, bit by bit, i'll push my body towards all that keeps me awake.

boy, only you stand in the way of you, boy,
i whisper, *is today the day you get idle hands dirty?*

Poem for Lost Boys

Sorrow like a palm stretches over my heart,
sorrow so real i can taste it on my tongue –
chemistry of bile and ash,
which reminds me of his tongue on mine,

his holiness, the image of a god
soiling earthen vessels with his vile hands,
a god breaking boys with kisses,

boys who become lost in their own skin,
who know pain so raw like needles dancing
over the face of a fresh wound.

Lullaby of Fire

When fire dances with a crazed appetite,
he eats everything into destruction,
like a brood of termites feasting on wood –
a city knows this, that when fire visits,
all that is left are crumbled pillars of ash.
When fire cuddles, when he romances a skin,
his kisses sting the flesh.
Say fire snuggles a woman & her child,
baptises them till their flesh becomes a burnt offering.

In the air is a marriage of odours –
of bodies & goods;
a man watches as his estates succumb
to the lullaby of flame;
a woman dances to the song of agony –
she slaps her thighs with her hands,
stomps the ground with her feet as
her wares are razed to ashes.
A house will mourn tonight,
for father is trapped in the inferno.

A city crumbles when she has thieves for princes;
she wails when the stomach of her
leaders bulge with state budget –
say fire went mad & firefighters couldn't
tame it in its wake,
for equipment funds were looted.
Madmen politicised the grief of a city,
threw pebbles of blame across parties
while headlines carried the name of a city:
Onitsha – Woman, child, others die in tanker fire

In Search of Peace

a man can be lost in his own home,
a stranger to his wife and sons.
a man may know of worlds within himself,
worlds he is running away from.
so he peels his skin with the mouth of broken things –
things broken like him.

a man may only be at home in darkness, in silence,
in solitude, like a monk in meditation,
only that daemons ravage his mind,
whispering thoughts darker than the shade of night.

a man may have enemies beyond the veil of earth,
enemies with AK-47 stooped over the ridges of his mind,
aiming at him –
and so this man will run,
run away, leaving his skin behind.

On the Cliff of Mother's Tongue

I'm a withering tree,
each thimbleful of air I sip is a ball of nails rolling down
my lung –
why my dreams are paperweight.
The pains that set on my body every dusk launch me
into visions of the Reaper with his sickle, reaping his
harvest.

Mother's eyes betray the question hanging on
the cliff of her tongue whenever she tends to my skin –
melanin fading like over-washed linen:
"Death, when will it be?"
It's her prayer for peace.

ABOUT THE AUTHOR

Adeola Juwon Gbalajobi is a Nigerian poet, ghostwriter and a connoisseur of Afro music. He believes in the healing power of words and the sheer beauty of poetry. His works have been published on various literary platforms. *Ellipsis* is his debut poetry collection.

Adeola writes from Lagos, Nigeria.

Author's Note

Thank you for the time you have taken to read this book. I hope you enjoyed the poems in it.

If you loved the book and have a minute to spare, I would appreciate a short review on the page or site where you bought it. I greatly appreciate your help in promoting my work. Reviews from readers like you make a huge difference in helping new readers choose the book.

Thank you!
Adeola Juwon Gbalajobi

www.ingramcontent.com/pod-product-compliance
Lightning Source LLC
Chambersburg PA
CBHW021452080526
44588CB00009B/817